Andy's Animal Alphabet Almanac

By Andy Crocker

All profits from the sale of this book will be donated to the
North Alabama Zoological Society (NALZS)

Book 1
Beginner

All poems in this book follow the
rhyme scheme of
"Twinkle, Twinkle, Little Star"

A IS FOR ALLIGATOR

American Alligator – Gulf Breeze Zoo
(Santa Rosa County, FL, USA)

Twinkle, twinkle, little eye,
How it watches us walk by.
Just below the surface keep;
Patient, silent, like asleep.
Open, though, the eye reveals
A malcontent our peace to steal.

Aa

4

Chinese Alligator – Sedgwick County Zoo (Wichita, KS, USA)

B is for Bear

Andean Bear – Baton Rouge Zoo
(Baton Rouge, LA, USA)

Grizzly, Polar, Black, and Sun–
Cute and cuddly, every one.
"Teddys" are our bedtime friends,
Hibernating in our dens.
Facing live, we're struck with awe
The massive power in one paw.

Bb

6

Grizzly Bear – Memphis Zoo (Memphis, TN, USA)

C IS FOR CAMEL

Long and lanky, slow of stride,
Through the desert, goes with pride.
Without water, good for days;
Heat and dryness cannot faze.
Loyal traveler, always true;
The question is: one hump or two?

Dromedary Camel – Chattanooga Zoo
(Chattanooga, TN, USA)

Cc

8

Bactrian Camel – Denver Zoo (Denver, CO, USA)

D IS FOR DOLPHIN

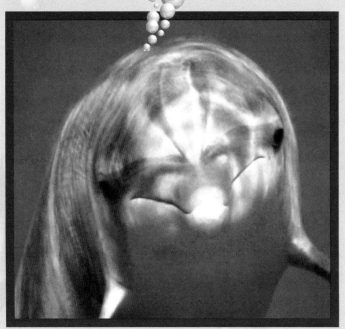

Common Bottlenose Dolphin – Indianapolis Zoo
(Indianapolis, IN, USA)

Swimming mammals, fast and sleek;
Clicks and whistles, how they speak.
Clever, friendly, they will play.
We are smarter, so we say;
Yes, they cannot live on ground,
But can humans see with sound?

Pacific White-sided Dolphin – Sea World San Antonio (San Antonio, TX, USA)

E is for Elephant

African Elephant — Zoo Knoxville
(Knoxville, TN, USA)

Gentle giant, quiet beast;
Grasses, fruit, and bark, her feast.
Her trunk can smell and lift and reach
And call to children, comfort, teach.
She's weighty, too, beyond her girth:
A mind with recall, wit, and mirth.

Ee

African Elephant – Birmingham Zoo (Birmingham, AL, USA)

F is for Flamingo

Eating, preening, sleeping bird,
Bent in shapes sometimes absurd.
Feathers soft with pinkish hue
Do create a lovely view.
But why sleep this way, we beg,
Standing on one tiny leg?

Caribbean Flamingo – Nashville Zoo
(Nashville, TN, USA)

Ff

14

Andean Flamingo – Memphis Zoo (Memphis, TN, USA)

G is for Giraffe

High up in the trees we gaze
Just to see him slowly graze.
On his lengthy neck are chic
Spots that fashion him unique.
Pardon when he needs to use
His ha lf an hour's daily snooze.

Gg

Reticulated Giraffe – Gulf Breeze Zoo
(Santa Rosa County, FL, USA)

Reticulated Giraffe – Monarto Safari Park (Monarto, South Australia, Australia)

H is for Hippopotamus

Hippopotamus – Memphis Zoo
(Memphis, TN, USA)

She spends her life submerged and wet
Because her skin does not make sweat.
Her eyes and nose and ears above,
But hidden mouth we're mindful of.
Be careful not to make her fuss;
She's huge but runs faster than us.

Hh

Pygmy Hippopotamus – Montgomery Zoo (Montgomery, AL, USA)

I IS FOR IGUANA

Strong jaws, sharp teeth, and razor claws
As a rule would give us pause.
He eats only plants–don't fret–
In fact can be a friendly pet.
His tail can give a foe a whack
And can come off! But it grows back.

Rhinoceros Iguana – Chattanooga Zoo
(Chattanooga, TN, USA)

Ii

Fiji Banded Iguana – San Antonio Zoo (San Antonio, TX, USA)

J IS FOR JAGUAR

She stalks in beauty–orange fur
And black rosettes–without a stir.
Her spotted coat can fool the eyes
And stealthy moves can hypnotize.
But danger in her name is found:
"She who kills in single bound."

Jaguar – Montgomery Zoo
(Montgomery, AL, USA)

22

Jaguar – Chattanooga Zoo (Chattanooga, TN, USA)

K IS FOR KANGAROO

Red Kangaroo – Denver Zoo
(Denver, CO, USA)

A mother's love is warm and deep
Just like the pouch where joeys keep.
Born inside that built-in purse,
Young ones ride and sleep and nurse.
Protected, too, by feet that thump
And speed to safety with long jumps.

Kk

Western Gray Kangaroo – Adelaide Cleland Wildlife Park
(Adelaide, South Australia, Australia)

L is for Lion

Kings of jungles, macho men,
Rule all they survey from their dens.
Rippling muscles, flowing manes,
Roars that boom across the plains.
But when hunting for the feed
The men stay back; the females lead.

African Lion – Birmingham Zoo
(Birmingham, AL, USA)

African Lion – Smithsonian's National Zoo (Washington, DC, USA)

M is for Monkey

Some have tails that grab and clutch;
Others' tails don't do too much.
Some live in trees and eat just fruit;
Others munch whatever suits.
But one truth we can't escape:
With a tail, it's not an ape.

Howler Monkey – Birmingham Zoo
(Birmingham, AL, USA)

Mm

Golden Lion Tamarin – Smithsonian's National Zoo (Washington, DC, USA)

N is for Newt

Kaiser Newt – Dallas Zoo
(Dallas, TX, USA)

Born as larvae, then tadpoles,
Change to adults, little but whole.
Protected by their colors, bright;
Their bellies–red flags–scare on sight.
If still a rival gets too close
Their skin secretes a poison dose.

Emperor Newt – Smithsonian's National Zoo (Washington, DC, USA)

O IS FOR OWL

Horned Owl – Gulf Breeze Zoo
(Santa Rosa County, FL, USA)

Bird of prey with hunting skills
Has the perfect tools for kills:
Stealthy wings for silent flight;
Keen eyesight to see at night;
Hears precisely every sound;
Turns its head near full way 'round.

Oo

Burrowing Owl – Memphis Zoo (Memphis, TN, USA)

P is for Peacock

Indian Peafowl – Chattanooga Zoo
(Chattanooga, TN, USA)

The name belongs to just the males
Who have the colored, handsome tails.
Their patterns, widths, and color traits
Determine who choose them as mates.
As we admire, the painted arcs
Seem to stare back from eye-like marks.

Pp

Indian Peafowl – Baton Rouge Zoo (Baton Rouge, LA, USA)

Q IS FOR QUAIL

Northern Bobwhite Quail — National Aviary
(Pittsburgh, PA, USA)

Pheasant's brother is this sprite;
Pleasant feathers to invite.
Like a clicking castanet,
Crowing, hoping to duet.
Birds—however, to be found
Almost always on the ground.

Qq

Gambel's Quail – North Carolina Zoo (Asheboro, NC, USA)

R IS FOR ROOSTER

Comb and wattle are distinct;
Chicken male, with plumage inked.
Morning calls have earned him fame—
Shouts to all to stake his claim.
Lots of friends within the flock—
As long as they know it's his block.

Cuckoo Maran Rooster – North Georgia Wildlife Park
(Cleveland, GA, USA)

Rr

Old English Game Rooster – Gulf Breeze Zoo (Santa Rosa County, FL, USA)

S IS FOR SHEEP

If you had a little lamb
He could grow to be a ram.
On a farm, he'd be a source
Of wool that's fine, average, or course.
But who, pray tell, could give some milk
To you? A ewe that's of his ilk.

Karakul Sheep – Sedgwick County Zoo
(Wichita, KS, USA)

Shetliot Sheep – North Georgia Wildlife Park (Cleveland, GA, USA)

T is for Tiger

Bengal Tiger – Montgomery Zoo
(Montgomery, AL, USA)

He's the biggest cat worldwide;
Still his footsteps almost glide.
Known for black and orange tints;
Stripes unique, like fingerprints.
Marks his territory well–
Leaves behind a musky smell.

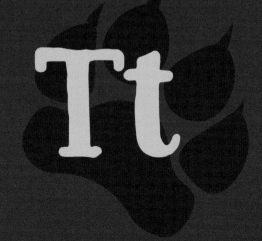

Tt

Sumatran Tiger – San Antonio Zoo (San Antonio, TX, USA)

U is for Urchin

Pencil Urchin – Monterey Bay Aquarium
(Monterey, CA, USA)

Lives on ocean reef and rock.
Feet with suckers help her lock
Tight to drill a place to dwell–
Hidden–dangers to repel.
Spikes are there for her welfare;
Some are venom-filled–beware!

Uu

44

Purple Urchin – Georgia Aquarium (Atlanta, GA, USA)

45

V is for Vulture

Seeing things rotting or dead
Won't make us think of getting fed;
But she will by no means eschew,
As part of nature's clean-up crew.
In fact, this thought may make us groan:
Her diet's based of mostly bones.

King Vulture – Fort Worth Zoo
(Fort Worth, TX, USA)

46

Black Vulture – Chattanooga Zoo (Chattanooga, TN, USA)

W IS FOR WOLF

Red Wolf – Zoo Knoxville
(Knoxville, TN, USA)

Awesome hunters, lethal pack,
Work together as they track.
Ears can pass a ten-mile test;
Smell one hundred times our best.
Stalk for days before they dine.
Hard to think they are canines.

Ww

Gray Wolf – Memphis Zoo (Memphis, TN, USA)

X is for X-Ray Fish

X-Ray Tetra – Denver Zoo
(Denver, CO, USA)

Hard to say which should enchant–
What we see or what we can't.
Backbone through the skin is clear...
Then a shimmer–disappears.
Eggs observed before they spawn
In the river Amazon.

Xx

X-Ray Tetra – Denver Zoo (Denver, CO, USA)

Y IS FOR YAK

Tibetan Royal Yak – North Georgia Wildlife Park
(Cleveland, GA, USA)

Mountain living is the norm.
Thick and woolly to stay warm.
Minus forty? Not too low.
She doesn't mind the heavy snow.
Prized for fur and milk and meat
And dung, that's burned to create heat.

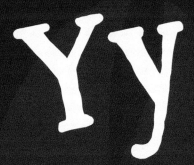

Yy

Domestic Yak – Tupelo Buffalo Park & Zoo (Tupelo, MS, USA)

Z IS FOR ZEBRA

Quickly known by black and white,
Patterns tell who's who on sight.
Designs can also be a ruse:
A herd of stripes, clustered, confuse.
But how to keep from being prey?
Sleep standing up, then run away.

Grevy's Zebra – Smithsonian's National Zoo
(Washington, DC, USA)

Zz

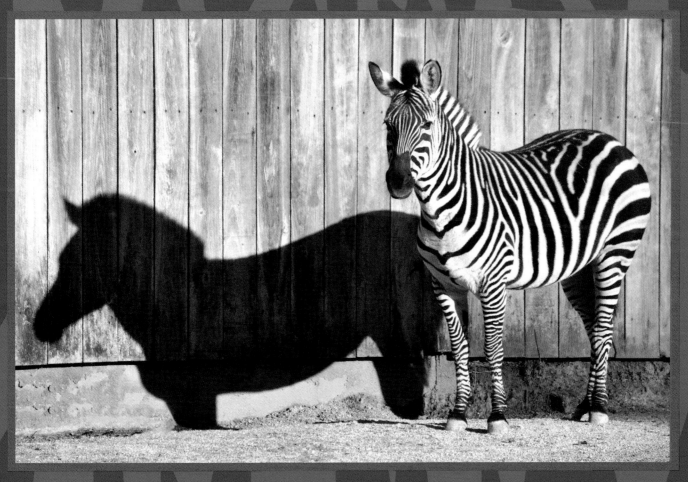

Grant's Zebra – Memphis Zoo (Memphis, TN, USA)

The End

Plains Zebra – Woodland Park Zoo (Seattle, WA, USA)

Acknowledgments

Thank you to the following zoos and aquariums for permitting the use of pictures of their animals in this book to benefit wildlife conservation, research, and education:

Adelaide Cleland Wildlife Park
Baton Rouge Zoo
Birmingham Zoo
Chattanooga Zoo
Dallas Zoo
Denver Zoo
Fort Worth Zoo
Georgia Aquarium
Gulf Breeze Zoo
Indianapolis Zoo
Zoo Knoxville
Memphis Zoo
Monarto Safari Park

Monterey Bay Aquarium
Montgomery Zoo
Nashville Zoo
National Aviary
North Carolina Zoo
North Georgia Wildlife Park
Pittsburgh Zoo and PPG Aquarium
San Antonio Zoo
Sea World San Antonio
Sedgwick County Zoo
Smithsonian's National Zoo
Tupelo Buffalo Park & Zoo
Woodland Park Zoo

About the Author

Creating this book allowed Andy Crocker to combine into a single project several of his passions: poetry, photography, and zoos. He is trained and works as an engineer, but he enjoys being a "Renaissance Man." He has always been interested in the arts and particularly in poetry. When digital photography entered the mainstream, his interest in photography began. He started out photographing landscapes and travel destinations—and he still enjoys them both—but he eventually developed a love of photographing animals. He has visited over 75 zoos and aquariums and wildlife reserves around the world, and he visits new ones whenever he can. He is a member of the Board of Directors for the North Alabama Zoological Society (NALZS), which is developing a new zoo for the Huntsville, Alabama/Tennessee Valley area.

For his "day job," Crocker is a real-life rocket scientist. He has had the opportunity to work on many incredible projects, including serving as manager of the Human Landing System, where he led a diverse team in the development of a system to transport crew and cargo to and from the Moon.

Crocker earned undergraduate degrees in Aerospace Engineering and Multidisciplinary Studies from N.C. State University and graduate degrees in engineering and management from the University of Florida and Rensselaer Polytechnic Institute. In addition to NALZS, he has served on Boards for the Huntsville Chapter of the National Space Club and the Sci-Quest Hands-on Science Center.

He lives in North Alabama, where he and his wife have raised two children.

59